Copyright ©2025 Barbara De Simon

Published in Windsor, Ontario, Canada by Barbara De Simon and makeyourselfready.com - A Kingdom ministry teaching women to know their Bridegroom intimately and equipping them to fulfill their call on the earth.

All rights reserved. This book is protected by the copyright laws of Canada. No part of this publication may be reproduced, stored in a retrieval system, or transmitted in any form or by any means—electronic, mechanical, photocopy, recording or any other—except for brief quotations, without prior permission of the author/publisher.

Scripture quotations marked NKJV are from the New King James Version®. Copyright © 1982 by Thomas Nelson, Inc. Used by permission. All rights reserved.

Scripture quotations marked TPT are from The Passion Translation®. Copyright © 2017, 2018, 2020 by Passion & Fire Ministries, Inc. Used by permission. All rights reserved. ThePassionTranslation.com.

Cover and interior design by Barbara De Simon; cover image from iStock.com
Some interior images created in Canva
Some interior images by Emma and Mia Gauthier

ISBN: 978-1-7383840-4-4

Dedicated

To all the Pentecostal women roommates I met at Pioneer Camp Ontario in Huntsville back in 1989, who first introduced me to our supernatural God and His supernatural, powerful Holy Spirit.

Day One

Lord, you know everything there is to know about me. You perceive every movement of my heart and soul, and you understand my every thought before it even enters my mind.
(Psalms 139:1-2 TPT)

How does it make you feel knowing that God perceives and knows your every thought beforehand and knows the depths of your heart—every nook and cranny? How does it make you feel that you actually can't hide anything from Him and even that there could be things that He knows about your heart that maybe you don't? Perhaps it makes you a bit nervous, like it does me. I don't want Him to know EVERYTHING! But He does. He saw what we have done in our worst moments, and He saw what others have done to us too. He didn't miss a thing. However, you can exhale and let out a big sigh of relief because the good news is, He still loves us all the same. There is nothing that will cause Him to reject us—nothing we could do or experience that would cause Him to turn away and not absolutely long to be with us every day.

Our Pappa God is good. He is extraordinarily good and not like our earthly fathers at all. For some, this truth is incredibly meaningful and others not so much, but wherever you stand, know that Pappa God's heart is full of mercy and grace for all your mistakes and all your wounds. He is always available when we need Him, sitting on the edge of His seat waiting for us to come to Him.

It's very possible He is saying to you today:

"Daughter, you are mine and I am yours. No matter what you've been through and no matter what you've done, I will always love you. There is nothing you can do that would cause Me to love you more and nothing you could do to make Me love you less. My love for you is perfect at every moment. Release yourself from every wrong and every weakness and receive my love and forgiveness today. It is waiting for you to break open and pour over your own head. Take from me, anoint yourself, and watch all your shame and guilt wash away."

Prayer

"Thank you, Lord, for Your love. Holy Spirit, what else do you want to show me?"

Revelation

Did Holy Spirit show you a picture? If so, describe it and write what it means to you. Do you know a scripture that supports what you saw? If not, ask the Holy Spirit to give you one. Did Holy Spirit whisper something to you? If so, write it down and journal how it makes you feel.

Day One

Respond
What do you want to say to God in response?

_____
_____
_____
_____
_____
_____
_____

End of Day Inventory
What did you struggle with today? Journal about it.

_____
_____
_____
_____
_____
_____
_____
_____

"Now it's time to be made new by every revelation that's been given to you. And to be transformed as you embrace the glorious Christ-within as your new life and live in union with him! For God has re-created you all over again in his perfect righteousness, and you now belong to him in the realm of true holiness. So discard every form of dishonesty and lying so that you will be known as one who always speaks the truth, for we all belong to one another. But don't let the passion of your emotions lead you to sin! *Don't let anger control you or be fuel for revenge, not for even a day.* Don't give the slanderous accuser, the Devil, an opportunity to manipulate you!" (Ephesians 4:23-27 TPT, emphasis added)

What made you angry today? Write out a prayer and tell God about it.

Day One

How did you respond when you were angry? Do you need to apologize to someone and ask for forgiveness?

_____

_____

_____

_____

_____

_____

_____

If there was a person that you felt angry at, ask Holy Spirit to show you their heart. Did Holy Spirit show you something? Has this helped you to feel compassion for that person? Journal about your experience as you prayed.

_____

_____

_____

_____

_____

_____

Day One

Final Prayer

"Lord, I confess that I reacted in anger toward...

_____

_____

_____

My behaviour was unacceptable. And I'm sorry. I repent. Please forgive me. I reject shame and choose to forgive myself. I receive Your forgiveness, Lord, in its fullness. I choose to forgive...

_____

_____

For...

_____

_____

_____

_____

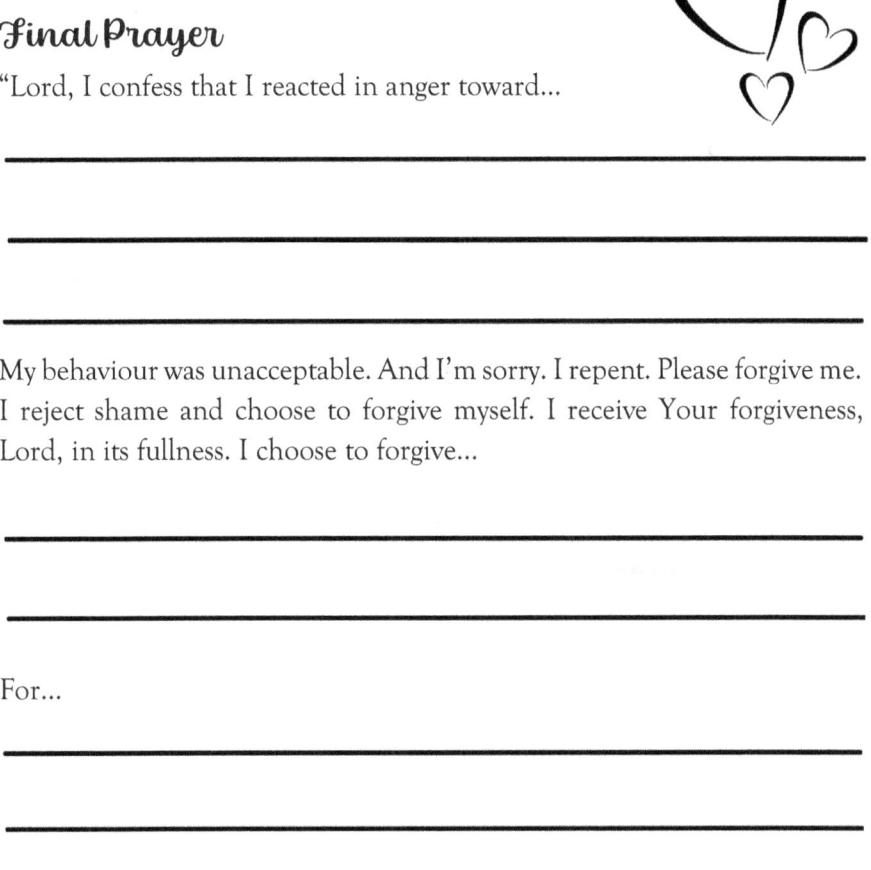

I fully release them to You, God, to be their righteous judge. I renounce anger, shame, bitterness, slander, and unforgiveness in Jesus' name and I command them to leave right now, on my natural breathing. [Breathe deep and in faith believe that any spirits attached to your anger are leaving.] Father God, fill me with Your Holy Spirit. Fill every place in me that was vacated. Thank You for Your faithfulness to me. In Jesus' name, amen."

Continue to repent in the same manner as above, for anything else the Holy Spirit puts on your heart.

Notes

Day Two

You are so intimately aware of me, Lord. You read my heart like an open book and you know all the words I'm about to speak before I even start a sentence! You know every step I will take before my journey even begins. (Psalms 139:3-4 TPT)

This is the essence of intimacy—to know and to be known exactly as you are, deeply and completely. In any relationship the goal is to get to know the heart of the other person until you're able to finish their sentences and predict what they will say or do in any given situation. This is how God knows you and this is how God wants you to know Him.

As in any relationship, we get to know God's heart by spending *quality* and *quantity* time with Him in worship and conversation (prayer), reading His Word (the Bible), walking with Him throughout our day, and discerning His presence with us all the time. As we practice these things, we will get to know His voice better and we will grow in intimacy with Him; we will go from being servants and acquaintances to being friends, from being friends to being best friends, from best friends to being deeply in love, and then finally to being one, as a bride is with her Bridegroom, in deep intimacy. That's our goal. To know Him and to be known by Him. To behold Him and to be beheld by Him, with no distance between us.

It's very possible He is saying to you today:

"Daughter, I know all there is to know about you, and I choose to love you, just as you are. I see the end from the beginning, and in My plans, I have accounted for all your mistakes even before any of them have happened. Nothing takes Me by surprise. Your mistakes do not change the plans I have for you—My plans for your good, to prosper you and not to harm you, to give you hope and a future. Life will not be without challenges, but I promise to be with you through them all as you abide in Me and trust Me. You are my heart's desire, and I adore you as a husband adores his bride. I will take care of you and defend you when needed."

Prayer

"Thank you, Lord, for Your encouragement and care. Holy Spirit, what else do you want to show me?"

Revelation

Did Holy Spirit show you a picture? If so, describe it and write what it means to you. Do you know a scripture that supports what you saw? If not, ask the Holy Spirit to give you one. Did Holy Spirit whisper something to you? If so, write it down and journal how it makes you feel.

Day Two

Respond
What do you want to say to God in response?

_____

_____

_____

_____

_____

_____

_____

End of Day Inventory
What did you struggle with today? Journal about it.

_____

_____

_____

_____

_____

_____

_____

Walking with The Spirit

_____
_____
_____
_____
_____
_____

What made you angry today? Write out a prayer and tell God about it.

_____
_____
_____
_____
_____
_____
_____
_____
_____
_____
_____

Day Two

How did you respond when you were angry? Do you need to apologize to someone and ask for forgiveness?

_____

_____

_____

_____

_____

_____

If there was a person that you felt angry at, ask Holy Spirit to show you their heart. Did Holy Spirit show you something? Has this helped you to feel compassion for that person? Journal about your experience as you prayed.

_____

_____

_____

_____

_____

Final Prayer

"Lord, I confess that I reacted in anger toward...

_____

_____

_____

My behaviour was unacceptable. And I'm sorry. I repent. Please forgive me. I choose to forgive myself and I receive Your forgiveness in its fullness. I choose to forgive...

_____

_____

For...

_____

_____

_____

_____

I fully release them to You, God, to be their righteous judge. I renounce anger and unforgiveness in Jesus' name and I command them to leave on my natural breathing right now. [Breathe deep and in faith believe that any spirits attached to your anger are leaving.] Father God, fill me with Your Holy Spirit. Fill every place in me that is now vacant. Thank You for Your faithfulness to me. In Jesus' name, amen."

Continue to repent in the same manner as above, for anything else the Holy Spirit puts on your heart.

Day Three

You've gone into my future to prepare the way, and in kindness you follow behind me to spare me from the harm of my past. You have laid your hand on me! This is just too wonderful, deep, and incomprehensible! Your understanding of me brings me wonder and strength. (Psalms 139:5-6 TPT)

What a wonderful thought! With so much anxiety about our future due to what has already happened in our past, God Almighty, hedges about us, in front and behind, even going into our future preparing the way and creating a plan for our restoration. This does not mean that our future will be perfect, as Jesus tells us in John 16:33 that we will have trouble or tribulation in the world. However, He also tells us that we can have peace in the midst of it because He has overcome the world on our behalf. In other words, we can have courage because He has already made a way for us to overcome any trouble and tribulation we face. His hand is upon us! Nothing that happens to us takes Him by surprise or is out of His control to redeem and turn around for our good (Romans 8:28). The scope of the revelation of how He works in our lives really is beyond our comprehension, but we can ask Him to help us understand. His ways are higher than ours and His thoughts beyond our thoughts. All glory to God!

It's very possible He is saying to you today:

"Daughter, I understand you completely. Nothing about you is beyond my knowledge or understanding. I know everything about your future, and I have already planned how and when to bring you healing and restoration. Remain in Me. Don't try to do any of it without Me. I am your life source. When you abide in Me and trust Me, you will have the strength and the power to overcome life's challenges. Stay connected to My voice and heed my instruction no matter how unconventional it may seem for I know things you don't. Trust Me. I am for you, always."

Prayer

"Thank you, Lord, for Your encouragement and care. Holy Spirit, what else do you want to show me?"

Revelation

Did Holy Spirit show you a picture? If so, describe it and write what it means to you. Do you know a scripture that supports what you saw? If not, ask the Holy Spirit to give you one. Did Holy Spirit whisper something to you? If so, write it down and journal how it makes you feel.

Day Three

Respond
What do you want to say to God in response?

_____
_____
_____
_____
_____
_____
_____

End of Day Inventory
What did you struggle with today? Journal about it.

_____
_____
_____
_____
_____
_____
_____

_____

_____

_____

_____

_____

_____

What made you angry today? Write out a prayer and tell God about it.

_____

_____

_____

_____

_____

_____

_____

_____

_____

_____

Day Three

How did you respond when you were angry? Do you need to apologize to someone and ask for forgiveness?

_____

_____

_____

_____

_____

_____

If there was a person that you felt angry at, ask Holy Spirit to show you their heart. Did Holy Spirit show you something? Has this helped you to feel compassion for that person? Journal about your experience as you prayed.

_____

_____

_____

_____

_____

Final Prayer

"Lord, I confess that I reacted in anger toward...

_____

_____

_____

My behaviour was unacceptable. And I'm sorry. I repent. Please forgive me. I choose to forgive myself and I receive Your forgiveness in its fullness. I choose to forgive...

_____

_____

For...

_____

_____

_____

I fully release them to You, God, to be their righteous judge. I renounce anger and unforgiveness in Jesus' name and I command them to leave on my natural breathing right now. [Breathe deep and in faith believe that any spirits attached to your anger are leaving.] Father God, fill me with Your Holy Spirit. Fill every place in me that is now vacant. Thank You for Your faithfulness to me. In Jesus' name, amen."

Continue to repent in the same manner as above, for anything else the Holy Spirit puts on your heart.

Day Four

Where could I go from your Spirit? Where could I run and hide from your face? If I go up to heaven, you're there! If I go down to the realm of the dead, you're there too!
(Psalms 139:7-8 TPT)

It is so true. There is not a spot where God is not! His presence is everywhere we go; He never leaves us, forgets about us or abandons us. Even if we are in a pit, and even if we are there because of our own choices, God never abandons us. He waits and gently invites us back to Him when we're ready.

Have you ever tried to hide from God? Yes? Me too. We seem to allow shame to convince us that the Lord won't receive us, that He'll be disappointed in us, perhaps scold us, lecture us, and even reject us. But these are all lies designed to keep us from God and His healing power and love. Wherever we find ourselves, He is there. When you think you're running away or hiding, you're actually not. He's running right along side you and sees you right where you are. Just as Adam and Eve couldn't hide from God, neither can we.

It's very possible God is saying to you today:

> *"Daughter, don't run away from Me, run to Me. My arms are open wide to receive you, without punishment. There is no need to fear My care. Yes, I may discipline you, but it is not the type of discipline you are used to. I discipline out of love, and I correct My children gently—never harshly. There is no need to try and avoid My correction or My guidance. I will never be disappointed in you or be mad at you. My heart may grieve for you and what you are enduring perhaps because of the natural consequences of your sin, but my heart is always to heal you, help you, teach you, and restore you back to My original design and intent for your life. Trust Me. I will never reject you, ignore you, or hurt you. You are my beloved daughter, and I paid the dearest price to be with you."*

Prayer

"Thank you, Lord, for Your encouragement and care. Holy Spirit, what else do you want to show me?"

Revelation

Did Holy Spirit show you a picture? If so, describe it and write what it means to you. Do you know a scripture that supports what you saw? If not, ask the Holy Spirit to give you one. Did Holy Spirit whisper something to you? If so, write it down and journal how it makes you feel.

Day Four

Respond
What do you want to say to God in response?

_____

_____

_____

_____

_____

_____

_____

End of Day Inventory
What did you struggle with today? Journal about it.

_____

_____

_____

_____

_____

_____

_____

Walking with The Spirit

What made you angry today? Write out a prayer and tell God about it.

Day Four

How did you respond when you were angry? Do you need to apologize to someone and ask for forgiveness?

_____

_____

_____

_____

_____

_____

If there was a person that you felt angry at, ask Holy Spirit to show you their heart. Did Holy Spirit show you something? Has this helped you to feel compassion for that person? Journal about your experience as you prayed.

_____

_____

_____

_____

_____

Final Prayer

"Lord, I confess that I reacted in anger toward...

_____

_____

_____

My behaviour was unacceptable. And I'm sorry. I repent. Please forgive me. I choose to forgive myself and I receive Your forgiveness in its fullness. I choose to forgive...

_____

_____

For...

_____

_____

_____

I fully release them to You, God, to be their righteous judge. I renounce anger and unforgiveness in Jesus' name and I command them to leave on my natural breathing right now. [Breathe deep and in faith believe that any spirits attached to your anger are leaving.] Father God, fill me with Your Holy Spirit. Fill every place in me that is now vacant. Thank You for Your faithfulness to me. In Jesus' name, amen."

Continue to repent in the same manner as above, for anything else the Holy Spirit puts on your heart.

Notes

Day Five

*If I fly with wings into the shining dawn, you're there! If I fly
into the radiant sunset, you're there waiting! Wherever I go,
your hand will guide me; your strength will empower me.*
(Psalms 139:9-10 TPT)

For consistency's sake, I have quoted the Passion Translation above, and it's beautiful. It highlights both sunrise and sunset, the beginning of our day to the end, to be good, positive places to be with Jesus, and it reminds us that we were created to fly in His presence. Like great bookends that support everything in-between and hold everything together, we begin and end our day with Him under His great power and guidance.

Other versions, however, of the same passage, make me wonder, have you ever had a day when at the end of it, you were so far away from where you began or wanted to be, you wondered if His presence had left you for good? You began your day with a devotional, in His presence, positive, but by the end you were dwelling in the uttermost parts of the sea, discouraged, so far removed from that positive place with Him. The good news is He will never leave you, no matter where you go or what you do. The Lord's mercy is so far reaching we can never go far enough west or east to escape it. The moment we reach out to Him in repentance, He forgives (1 John 1:9). How far is it from the farthest east to the farthest west? Not far enough to separate us from His love but far enough that our sin is removed from us forever. "As far as the east is from the west, so far has He removed our transgressions from us" (Psalm 103:12 NKJV). Praise the Lord! His guidance, strength and power are always with us.

It's very possible He is saying to you today:

*"Daughter, I've got you. I will meet you wherever you are, whether it be at
sunrise or sunset, in the east or the west, in encouragement or
discouragement; you are mine and I'm here for you. I will lift you up and
restore your heart through forgiveness and mercy. My hand is always on
you for your good, guiding you, directing you, correcting you and
encouraging you through life's trials. Trust Me."*

Prayer

"Thank you, Lord, for Your encouragement and care. Holy Spirit, what else do you want to show me?"

Revelation

Did Holy Spirit show you a picture? If so, describe it and write what it means to you. Do you know a scripture that supports what you saw? If not, ask the Holy Spirit to give you one. Did Holy Spirit whisper something to you? If so, write it down and journal how it makes you feel.

_____

_____

_____

_____

_____

_____

_____

_____

_____

_____

_____

_____

_____

Day Five

Respond
What do you want to say to God in response?

_____
_____
_____
_____
_____
_____
_____

End of Day Inventory
What did you struggle with today? Journal about it.

_____
_____
_____
_____
_____
_____
_____

Walking with The Spirit

_____

What made you angry today? Write out a prayer and tell God about it.

Day Five

How did you respond when you were angry? Do you need to apologize to someone and ask for forgiveness?

_____

_____

_____

_____

_____

_____

If there was a person that you felt angry at, ask Holy Spirit to show you their heart. Did Holy Spirit show you something? Has this helped you to feel compassion for that person? Journal about your experience as you prayed.

_____

_____

_____

_____

_____ MERCY

Final Prayer

"Lord, I confess that I reacted in anger toward...

_____

_____

_____

My behaviour was unacceptable. And I'm sorry. I repent. Please forgive me. I choose to forgive myself and I receive Your forgiveness in its fullness. I choose to forgive...

_____

_____

For...

_____

_____

_____

_____

I fully release them to You, God, to be their righteous judge. I renounce anger and unforgiveness in Jesus' name and I command them to leave on my natural breathing right now. [Breathe deep and in faith believe that any spirits attached to your anger are leaving.] Father God, fill me with Your Holy Spirit. Fill every place in me that is now vacant. Thank You for Your faithfulness to me. In Jesus' name, amen."

Continue to repent in the same manner as above, for anything else the Holy Spirit puts on your heart.

Day Six

*It's impossible to disappear from you or to ask the darkness
to hide me, for your presence is everywhere, bringing
light into my night. There is no such thing as darkness
with you. The night, to you, is as bright as the day; there's no
difference between the two. (Psalms 139:11-12 TPT)*

One of the greatest truths I cling to is this: light is always greater than darkness and light always dispels darkness. Light comes in and darkness flees. So, with that being said, because God's presence is always with us and God is light, darkness should not even exist in our experience. Right? Well, if we're being honest, we would admit that there *are* times when we feel like we're surrounded by darkness, like we're drowning in a pit of heaviness and despair. Why is that? Are we misunderstanding the scripture? No. Scripture is clear, and our understanding is accurate, but if we lose our awareness of God's presence and allow our emotions to become overwhelmed with lies and half-truths, our focus shifts to the darkness that wants to deceive, consume and overtake. Our job is to train our mind and emotions to focus on the right things like truth, hope, love, peace, and joy and not give place to the darkness. When darkness touches us, we need to run to the Father quickly, and cast all our cares, our hurts, and our pain on the Him and let Him rescue us with His light. Discipline yourself to focus on God's ever-abiding presence, even amid trials and difficult circumstances; ask Him, "Lord, open my spiritual eyes and show me where You are. I want to see You!"

It's very possible God is saying to you today:

*"Daughter, don't be distracted by the world and its chaos. Focus on Me
and My goodness. Focus on My love for You that never wains. Focus on
My presence with you. I will never leave you nor abandon you. You are
mine. My strength and My power are with you to overcome every obstacle
and every lie. Read My Word every day so you never lose sight of it.
I'm here for You every moment of every day.
Call out to Me and I will answer."*

Prayer

"Thank you, Lord, for Your encouragement and care. Holy Spirit, what else do you want to show me?"

Revelation

Did Holy Spirit show you a picture? If so, describe it and write what it means to you. Do you know a scripture that supports what you saw? If not, ask the Holy Spirit to give you one. Did Holy Spirit whisper something to you? If so, write it down and journal how it makes you feel.

_____

_____

_____

_____

_____

_____

_____

_____

_____

_____

_____

_____

_____

_____

Day Six

Respond
What do you want to say to God in response?

_____
_____
_____
_____
_____
_____
_____
_____

End of Day Inventory
What did you struggle with today? Journal about it.

_____
_____
_____
_____
_____
_____
_____

Walking with The Spirit

What made you angry today? Write out a prayer and tell God about it.

Day Six

How did you respond when you were angry? Do you need to apologize to someone and ask for forgiveness?

_____

_____

_____

_____

_____

_____

If there was a person that you felt angry at, ask Holy Spirit to show you their heart. Did Holy Spirit show you something? Has this helped you to feel compassion for that person? Journal about your experience as you prayed.

_____

_____

_____

_____

_____

_____

Final Prayer

"Lord, I confess that I reacted in anger toward...

_____

_____

_____

My behaviour was unacceptable. And I'm sorry. I repent. Please forgive me. I choose to forgive myself and I receive Your forgiveness in its fullness. I choose to forgive...

_____

_____

For...

_____

_____

_____

_____

I fully release them to You, God, to be their righteous judge. I renounce anger and unforgiveness in Jesus' name and I command them to leave on my natural breathing right now. [Breathe deep and in faith believe that any spirits attached to your anger are leaving.] Father God, fill me with Your Holy Spirit. Fill every place in me that is now vacant. Thank You for Your faithfulness to me. In Jesus' name, amen."

Continue to repent in the same manner as above, for anything else the Holy Spirit puts on your heart.

Day Seven

You formed my innermost being, shaping my delicate inside and my intricate outside, and wove them all together in my mother's womb. I thank you, God, for making me so mysteriously complex! Everything you do is marvellously breathtaking. It simply amazes me to think about it! How thoroughly you know me, Lord! (Psalms 139:13-14 TPT)

Did you know that there is divine power in speaking (out loud) God's Word over yourself? This is called making a "declaration." A declaration is a "formal or explicit statement or announcement"[1] to every power, good and bad, in the spirit realm and it can shift you, your experience, and even your circumstances. Proverbs 18:21 says, "Death and life are in the power of the tongue, And those who love it will eat its fruit" (NKJV). Hebrews 4:12 says, "For the word of God is living and powerful, and sharper than any two-edged sword, piercing even to the division of soul and spirit..." (NKJV). Isaiah 55:11 says, "So shall My word be that goes forth from My mouth; It shall not return to Me void, But it shall accomplish what I please, And it shall prosper in the thing for which I sent it" (NKJV). Declare over yourself today and every day, "Thank you God that YOU alone formed my innermost being. YOU shaped me inside and out. YOU knit me together in my mother's womb and You don't make mistakes. I am YOUR workmanship (Eph.2:10) and everything YOU do is marvellous and wonderful." When you declare this truth out loud enough times and believe it, your opinion about yourself will heal AND it could even begin to heal your physiology. Why? Because it can undo whatever the enemy tried to do in the womb, all those years ago. Don't be concerned about the passage of time; our God owns time. He transcends time. He is everywhere and in every moment of time all at once. I challenge you today to, "Trust in the Lord with all your heart, And *lean not on your own understanding;* In all your ways acknowledge Him, And He shall direct your paths" (Proverbs 3:5-6 NKJV, italics added). God's ways tend to go beyond our own understanding. That's why we need to walk by faith!

Day Seven

Prayer

"Thank you, Lord, for Your encouragement and care. Holy Spirit, what else do you want to show me?"

Revelation

Did Holy Spirit show you a picture? If so, describe it and write what it means to you. Do you know a scripture that supports what you saw? If not, ask the Holy Spirit to give you one. Did Holy Spirit whisper something to you? If so, write it down and journal how it makes you feel.

_____

_____

_____

_____

_____

_____

_____

_____

_____

_____

_____

_____

_____

_____

_____

_____

_____

_____

_____

FATHER TO THE FATHERLESS

Respond

What do you want to say to God in response?

_____
_____
_____
_____
_____
_____
_____

End of Day Inventory

What did you struggle with today? Journal about it.

_____
_____
_____
_____
_____
_____
_____
_____

Walking with The Spirit

What made you angry today? Write out a prayer and tell God about it.

Day Seven

How did you respond when you were angry? Do you need to apologize to someone and ask for forgiveness?

_____

_____

_____

_____

_____

_____

_____

If there was a person that you felt angry at, ask Holy Spirit to show you their heart. Did Holy Spirit show you something? Has this helped you to feel compassion for that person? Journal about your experience as you prayed.

_____

_____

_____

_____

_____

_____

Day Seven

Final Prayer

"Lord, I confess that I reacted in anger toward...

_____

_____

_____

My behaviour was unacceptable. And I'm sorry. I repent. Please forgive me. I choose to forgive myself and I receive Your forgiveness in its fullness. I choose to forgive...

_____

_____

For...

_____

_____

_____

_____

I fully release them to You, God, to be their righteous judge. I renounce anger and unforgiveness in Jesus' name and I command them to leave on my natural breathing right now. [Breathe deep and in faith believe that any spirits attached to your anger are leaving.] Father God, fill me with Your Holy Spirit. Fill every place in me that is now vacant. Thank You for Your faithfulness to me. In Jesus' name, amen."

Continue to repent in the same manner as above, for anything else the Holy Spirit puts on your heart.

Notes

Day Eight

You even formed every bone in my body when you created me in the secret place; carefully, skillfully you shaped me from nothing to something. You saw who you created me to be before I became me! Before I'd ever seen the light of day, the number of days you planned for me were already recorded in your book. (Psalms 139:15-16 TPT)

Perhaps you've been thinking, *King David wrote this Psalm about himself, not me. I'm nothing like King David.* To which I would say, "Really?" Do you know that King David messed up big time? He was far from perfect. David sinned with Bathsheba, impregnated her, then sent her husband to the front-line of war, purposefully, so he would be killed in battle. Following the Prophet Nathan's confrontation of David's sin, David wrote Psalm 51. Here's verse 5, "Behold, I was brought forth in iniquity, and in sin my mother conceived me" (Ps. 51:5 NKJV). Yes, you read that correctly. King David is admitting here that he was conceived in sin, outside of a marital relationship, perhaps in adultery, we do not know exactly, but even though this is true, David still declares in faith that he was created by God Himself, that he was *not* a mistake. How many of you, reading this, have been burdened by the lie, "I was a mistake," or "I wasn't wanted?" The whole of Psalm 139 is not only true of King David, but true of you. The whole entire Bible is the Word of God over your life. It was intended to be like a mirror, showing you who you really are. James 1:23-24 says, "For if anyone is a hearer of the word and not a doer, he is like a man observing his natural face in a mirror; for he observes himself, goes away, and immediately forgets what kind of man he was" (NKJV). It's very possible God is saying to you today:

"Daughter, when I created you, I didn't "wing it." I planned it. I planned you intricately, so much so, that I had a blueprint of you before I ever began. I saw who you were before the flash of light that was your conception. I thought of you beforehand; you were not an afterthought or a mistake, but My intentional creation put on the earth at just the right time. All your days are ordained by Me."

Prayer

"Thank you, Lord, for Your encouragement and care. Holy Spirit, what else do you want to show me?"

Revelation

Did Holy Spirit show you a picture? If so, describe it and write what it means to you. Do you know a scripture that supports what you saw? If not, ask the Holy Spirit to give you one. Did Holy Spirit whisper something to you? If so, write it down and journal how it makes you feel.

_____

_____

_____

_____

_____

_____

_____

_____

_____

_____

_____

_____

_____

Respond

What do you want to say to God in response?

_____

_____

_____

_____

_____

_____

_____

End of Day Inventory

What did you struggle with today? Journal about it.

_____

_____

_____

_____

_____

_____

_____

What made you angry today? Write out a prayer and tell God about it.

Day Eight

How did you respond when you were angry? Do you need to apologize to someone and ask for forgiveness?

_____

_____

_____

_____

_____

_____

If there was a person that you felt angry at, ask Holy Spirit to show you their heart. Did Holy Spirit show you something? Has this helped you to feel compassion for that person? Journal about your experience as you prayed.

_____

_____

_____

_____

_____

_____

Final Prayer

"Lord, I confess that I reacted in anger toward...

_____

_____

_____

My behaviour was unacceptable. And I'm sorry. I repent. Please forgive me. I choose to forgive myself and I receive Your forgiveness in its fullness. I choose to forgive...

_____

_____

For...

_____

_____

_____

_____

I fully release them to You, God, to be their righteous judge. I renounce anger and unforgiveness in Jesus' name and I command them to leave on my natural breathing right now. [Breathe deep and in faith believe that any spirits attached to your anger are leaving.] Father God, fill me with Your Holy Spirit. Fill every place in me that is now vacant. Thank You for Your faithfulness to me. In Jesus' name, amen."

Continue to repent in the same manner as above, for anything else the Holy Spirit puts on your heart.

Day Nine

Every single moment you are thinking of me! How precious and wonderful to consider that you cherish me constantly in your every thought! O God, your desires toward me are more than the grains of sand on every shore! When I awake each morning, you're still with me. (Psalms 139:17-18 TPT)

There's that word "cherish." I remember when I was young, I longed to be "cherished" by someone. I thought perhaps when I got married, I would be "cherished" but it didn't happen until I gave my heart to Jesus. Jesus is the only One Who can meet all our emotional needs completely.

I'm not sure why that word stuck out to me, but the word "cherish" means to "protect and care for (someone) lovingly, hold (something) dear" (Oxford Languages, Google). I also get from Google that cherish means "to hold them dear and to love, protect, and care for them *tenderly*." I think in my mind when you "cherish" someone, you recognize their worth; you recognize that they are precious and need special care and protection. When I think of God cherishing us, I realize that it totally makes sense because He knows how fragile we really are and knows exactly how we need to be loved—with compassion, tenderness, and care. Not even a thought in God's mind is contrary to this kind of love. After searching blueletterbible.org I found that the original word translated "thought" also means "purpose." The purposes and desires for us and our lives in God's heart are innumerable and can't be counted; there is therefore no need to worry that He's forgotten about us. . . ever!

It's very possible God is saying to you today:

> "Daughter, there are so many good things I desire to accomplish in you and in your life, but first my greatest desire is to restore you back to My original blueprint—My original and perfect version of you. As you lean on Me and trust Me, I will orchestrate your healing like only I can with gentleness and compassion. My eye is always on you. I see you and I see all you've been through. But I do love it when you choose to tell me all about it. I love it when you share your heart with Me, even when it's raw and unfiltered."

Prayer

"Thank you, Lord, for Your encouragement and care. Holy Spirit, what else do you want to show me?"

Revelation

Did Holy Spirit show you a picture? If so, describe it and write what it means to you. Do you know a scripture that supports what you saw? If not, ask the Holy Spirit to give you one. Did Holy Spirit whisper something to you? If so, write it down and journal how it makes you feel.

Day Ninet

Respond
What do you want to say to God in response?

_____
_____
_____
_____
_____
_____
_____

Were I to count them, they would outnumber the grains of sand

End of Day Inventory

What did you struggle with today? Journal about it.

_____

_____

_____

_____

_____

_____

_____

_____

_____

_____

_____

_____

_____

Day Nine

What made you angry today? Write out a prayer and tell God about it.

_____

_____

_____

_____

_____

_____

_____

_____

_____

_____

_____

How did you respond when you were angry? Do you need to apologize to someone and ask for forgiveness?

_____

_____

_____

_____

If there was a person that you felt angry at, ask Holy Spirit to show you their heart. Did Holy Spirit show you something? Has this helped you to feel compassion for that person? Journal about your experience as you prayed.

_____
_____
_____
_____
_____
_____

Final Prayer

"Lord, I confess that I reacted in anger toward…

_____
_____
_____

My behaviour was unacceptable. And I'm sorry. I repent. Please forgive me. I choose to forgive myself and I receive Your forgiveness in its fullness. I choose to forgive…

_____
_____

Day Nine

For...

_____

_____

_____

_____

I fully release them to You, God, to be their righteous judge. I renounce anger and unforgiveness in Jesus' name and I command them to leave on my natural breathing right now. [Breathe deep and in faith believe that any spirits attached to your anger are leaving.] Father God, fill me with Your Holy Spirit. Fill every place in me that is now vacant. Thank You for Your faithfulness to me. In Jesus' name, amen."

Continue to repent in the same manner as above, for anything else the Holy Spirit puts on your heart.

HOW PRECIOUS ARE YOUR THOUGHTS, O GOD!

Notes

Day Ten

O God, come and slay these bloodthirsty, murderous men! For I cry out, "Depart from me, you wicked ones!" See how they blaspheme your sacred name and lift up themselves against you, but all in vain! (Psalms 139:19-20 TPT)

If you're thinking, *well that took a turn!* You're right. King David's beautiful Psalm of connection with the Lord came to an end as he allowed the frustration with his circumstances to surface. But that's okay! It's a great reminder that King David was only human—just like us.

God knows that we are only dust. He knows our struggle; He is familiar with our weakness. He lived it Himself here on earth. He is not surprised by our emotions and inability to keep them in check at times. The Lord is gracious and wants us to "unload" on Him so we can be free from it in our heart; just don't unload and leave. Stay. Wait for the Lord's response and His embrace which is sure to come. This is the beautiful part. As we trust Him not to chastise us or scold us, the Lord will begin to gently change our heart by revealing deep things to us that we couldn't possibly know apart from Him—deep things that begin to birth compassion and understanding for others. Remember how we can't hide anything from Him? So, we might as well be honest about how we really feel so Holy Spirit can help us. Do not be afraid and do not hide your true feelings. God can handle your messiness. Your frustration. Your anger and your pain.

It's very possible He is saying to you today:

> *"Daughter, share your heart with Me—all the nitty gritty, the beautiful and the ugly. I already know it's there, so trust Me. Telling Me about it brings it out of the secret places and into My light where I can illuminate and dispel it. This will bring great relief to your heart. There is no need to hang onto sadness or pain. Release it to Me and watch it melt away. You are the one I love. There is no need to strive and try to be better in your own strength. It is impossible for you to do on your own. Rest in Me. Rest in My love and in My care and you will be restored."*

Prayer

"Thank you, Lord, for Your encouragement and care. Holy Spirit, what else do you want to show me?"

Revelation

Did Holy Spirit show you a picture? If so, describe it and write what it means to you. Do you know a scripture that supports what you saw? If not, ask the Holy Spirit to give you one. Did Holy Spirit whisper something to you? If so, write it down and journal how it makes you feel.

_____

_____

_____

_____

_____

_____

_____

_____

_____

_____

_____

_____

Respond

What do you want to say to God in response?

_____

_____

_____

_____

_____

_____

_____

End of Day Inventory

What did you struggle with today? Journal about it.

_____

_____

_____

_____

_____

_____

_____

Walking with The Spirit

_____

_____

_____

_____

_____

_____

_____

What made you angry today? Write out a prayer and tell God about it.

_____

_____

_____

_____

_____

_____

_____

_____

_____

_____

Day Ten

How did you respond when you were angry? Do you need to apologize to someone and ask for forgiveness?

_____

_____

_____

_____

_____

GRACE

If there was a person that you felt angry at, ask Holy Spirit to show you their heart. Did Holy Spirit show you something? Has this helped you to feel compassion for that person? Journal about your experience as you prayed.

_____

_____

_____

_____

_____

Final Prayer

"Lord, I confess that I reacted in anger toward...

_____

_____

_____

My behaviour was unacceptable. And I'm sorry. I repent. Please forgive me. I choose to forgive myself and I receive Your forgiveness in its fullness. I choose to forgive...

_____

_____

For...

_____

_____

_____

_____

I fully release them to You, God, to be their righteous judge. I renounce anger and unforgiveness in Jesus' name and I command them to leave on my natural breathing right now. [Breathe deep and in faith believe that any spirits attached to your anger are leaving.] Father God, fill me with Your Holy Spirit. Fill every place in me that is now vacant. Thank You for Your faithfulness to me. In Jesus' name, amen."

Continue to repent in the same manner as above, for anything else the Holy Spirit puts on your heart.

Day Eleven

Lord, can't you see how I despise those who despise you? For I grieve when I see them rise up against you. I have nothing but complete hatred and disgust for them. Your enemies shall be my enemies! (Psalms 139:21-22 TPT)

It seems that King David's flesh continues to lead his prayer. . . for the moment, but we also need to remember that this is Old Testament, before the New Covenant of grace, provided through Christ. In the OT, people who stood in the way of God and His people were dealt with harshly through battle. But what can *we* take away from this?

David says to God, "I despise those who despise you," and while we may be tempted to despise people for their sin, we must remember that this side of the cross the hatred of those who sin is not how God wants us to respond. We are ALL guilty of sin! Including King David! So rather than see *people* as the enemy, we should remember who our *real* enemy is.[2] God does not despise people, but He does despise the devil who is the ultimate source of all sin. In Matthew 5:44, Jesus clearly tells us to love our enemies—those who hate us or do us wrong, and pray for those who persecute us, "that you may be children of your Father in heaven."

Have you ever felt hatred and disgust in your heart for someone? Me too. But the Lord encourages us to confess it to Him and allow Him to help us see people through His eyes of grace and forgiveness. Let's direct our indignation toward the devil instead and stand against his lies and temptation as we are instructed to in Ephesians 6. Let's dig deep and allow Jesus to help us forgive those who have hurt us.

It's very possible God is saying to you today:

"Daughter, those who have hurt you are hurting; they have not recovered from their own trials. Some have come to Me and others have not; it is their own choice. But you have come to Me; I have drawn you in. Because you have heard Me, and come to Me, I will pour out upon you My healing balm; even in the night season as you sleep, I will touch you and heal you."

Prayer

"Thank you, Lord, for Your encouragement and care. Holy Spirit, what else do you want to show me?"

Revelation

Did Holy Spirit show you a picture? If so, describe it and write what it means to you. Do you know a scripture that supports what you saw? If not, ask the Holy Spirit to give you one. Did Holy Spirit whisper something to you? If so, write it down and journal how it makes you feel.

_____

_____

_____

_____

_____

_____

_____

_____

_____

_____

_____

_____

_____

Day Eleven

Respond
What do you want to say to God in response?

_____

_____

_____

_____

_____

_____

_____

End of Day Inventory
What did you struggle with today? Journal about it.

_____

_____

_____

_____

_____

_____

_____

_____
_____
_____
_____
_____
_____

What made you angry today? Write out a prayer and tell God about it.

_____
_____
_____
_____
_____
_____
_____
_____
_____
_____
_____

Day Eleven

How did you respond when you were angry? Do you need to apologize to someone and ask for forgiveness?

_____

_____

_____

_____

MERCY

If there was a person that you felt angry at, ask Holy Spirit to show you their heart. Did Holy Spirit show you something? Has this helped you to feel compassion for that person? Journal about your experience as you prayed.

_____

_____

_____

_____

_____

Final Prayer

"Lord, I confess that I reacted in anger toward...

_____

_____

_____

My behaviour was unacceptable. And I'm sorry. I repent. Please forgive me. I choose to forgive myself and I receive Your forgiveness in its fullness. I choose to forgive...

_____

_____

For...

_____

_____

_____

I fully release them to You, God, to be their righteous judge. I renounce anger and unforgiveness in Jesus' name and I command them to leave on my natural breathing right now. [Breathe deep and in faith believe that any spirits attached to your anger are leaving.] Father God, fill me with Your Holy Spirit. Fill every place in me that is now vacant. Thank You for Your faithfulness to me. In Jesus' name, amen."

Continue to repent in the same manner as above, for anything else the Holy Spirit puts on your heart.

Day Twelve

God, I invite your searching gaze into my heart. Examine me through and through; find out everything that may be hidden within me. Put me to the test and sift through all my anxious cares. See if there is any path of pain I'm walking on, and lead me back to your glorious, everlasting way—the path that brings me back to you. (Psalms 139:23-24 TPT)

I love how King David finishes this with the perfect prayer. He invites God to search his heart and reveal anything wicked and anything not of Him. I also love how Brian Simmons (translator of The Passion Translation) uses the term "path of pain." So often it is pain in our heart that causes us to veer off track, away from the straight and narrow path that leads to life with God. It's the pain there that causes us to self-protect and self-medicate, turning to sinful coping mechanisms. Pain deep in our heart also causes us to be triggered which in turn can cause us to react badly to situations and people. It is *this* pain we must cast on the Lord, give to Him, and ask Him to heal. He will clean our wounds, dress them in His love, and touch them so that healing becomes our experience. This prayer needs to be added to our daily routine but not in a way that it becomes wrote or powerless, but heart-felt and sincere inviting God's power to transform us. Let's be ready to repent and turn away from anything God shows us when we ask. Repenting every day and keeping short accounts with God is the way to life everlasting.

It's very possible He is saying to you today:

"Daughter, the blood of My Son is enough for you. It still works today to cleanse you of any guilt and shame, renewing you to Me every day. But you must allow My cleansing and forgiveness to do its work. You must decide that even though you don't deserve My forgiveness, you will receive it in fullness and allow it to lift off your shoulders all guilt, shame, and condemnation. If I have decided that you are forgiven, who are you to decide otherwise? Are you God? No. I am God. And you are not. My love, you ARE forgiven and your sins ARE completely remitted in full. The price has been paid."

Prayer

"Thank you, Lord, for Your encouragement and care. Holy Spirit, what else do you want to show me?"

Revelation

Did Holy Spirit show you a picture? If so, describe it and write what it means to you. Do you know a scripture that supports what you saw? If not, ask the Holy Spirit to give you one. Did Holy Spirit whisper something to you? If so, write it down and journal how it makes you feel.

_____

_____

_____

_____

_____

_____

_____

_____

_____

_____

forgiven _____

_____

Day Twelve

Respond
What do you want to say to God in response?

_____

_____

_____

_____

_____

_____

_____

Search me, God, and know my heart, test me and know my anxious thoughts.

End of Day Inventory

What did you struggle with today? Journal about it.

_____

_____

_____

_____

_____

_____

_____

_____

_____

_____

_____

_____

Day Twelve

What made you angry today? Write out a prayer and tell God about it.

_____

_____

_____

_____

_____

_____

_____

_____

_____

_____

How did you respond when you were angry? Do you need to apologize to someone and ask for forgiveness?

_____

_____

_____

If there was a person that you felt angry at, ask Holy Spirit to show you their heart. Did Holy Spirit show you something? Has this helped you to feel compassion for that person? Journal about your experience as you prayed.

_____

_____

_____

_____

_____

_____

_____

Final Prayer

"Lord, I confess that I reacted in anger toward...

_____

_____

_____

My behaviour was unacceptable. And I'm sorry. I repent. Please forgive me. I choose to forgive myself and I receive Your forgiveness in its fullness. I choose to forgive...

_____

_____

Day Twelve

For...

_____

_____

_____

_____

I fully release them to You, God, to be their righteous judge. I renounce anger and unforgiveness in Jesus' name and I command them to leave on my natural breathing right now. [Breathe deep and in faith believe that any spirits attached to your anger are leaving.] Father God, fill me with Your Holy Spirit. Fill every place in me that is now vacant. Thank You for Your faithfulness to me. In Jesus' name, amen."

Continue to repent in the same manner as above, for anything else the Holy Spirit puts on your heart.

About the Author

Barbara Jane grew up in a family of five attending a Christian Science church until the age of eighteen when she left home and at the age of twenty-two the Lord, Jesus, called her into His fold. She has now never been so grateful for the transformation the Lord began in her life in that moment of revelation and salvation. It was a moment when everything clicked into place, and everything she knew about God became crystal clear and made sense; the revelation of Jesus Christ was the missing piece. The years that followed would prove to be life altering and internally transforming in many ways.

Through her thirty-six years of faith in Christ thus far, she has had to face and renounce many things that tainted her family-line like the antichrist spirit, the spirit of error and deception, lies, abuse in many forms, deep anger, hate, unforgiveness, bitter judgements, vows to self, disappointment, rejection, self-loathing, and despair. As she has walked out of agreement with darkness, breakthrough has been had in different areas of life including her ability to conceive and bear natural children. Because of the goodness and healing of the Lord, Barbara Jane and her husband, Al, had four amazing children—one beautiful girl and three handsome boys, who are now all thriving adults. In addition, she and Al now have a wonderful daughter-in-law who makes a lovely addition to their original four.

It is with great honor that Barbara Jane pours out to her readers the knowledge, wisdom, and understanding that the Lord has poured into her. And it is her prayer that the time, love, and effort she has put into her books brings about great blessing and transformation in the lives of others. There is nothing more gratifying to Barbara than being used of the Lord to assist the Bride of Christ in getting ready for her big day, finally becoming perfectly united with her bridegroom, Jesus Christ.

Barbara has written five other books you might be interested in. They are as follows:

1. *Barren No More: Prayer Strategy for Every Believer Experiencing Fertility Challenges*
2. *Key to Fertility: Rewriting Your Stories for Success in Conceiving and Birthing Babies*
3. *Sweet Sorrow: Surviving the Emotional Waves of Releasing Your Son to His Bride*
4. *Position Yourself for Healing: Finding the Sweet Spot Where Healing Becomes Reality*
5. *Spiritual Protection and Deliverance for our Children*
6. *Loved and Fully Surrendered*

All can be purchased on Amazon.

Watch for children's companion books to *Spiritual Protection and Deliverance for our Children* starring Alistair, who struggles with fear and anger, and *Identity Theft: Coming Back to the Perfect Intentions of God for My Life*. Coming Soon!

Acknowledgements

First and foremost, I want to thank the Holy Spirit, Jesus, and Father God for my life here *and* to come, for peace, for loving me perfectly, for always being with me, for their faithfulness, and for the wisdom they have imparted to me without fail. You are my first and most important love, always and forever.

As well, a huge and special thank you goes to the following individuals who have significantly poured life, wisdom, and encouragement into me over the years, equipped me in the gifts of the Spirit and helped me to walk in God's confidence knowing who I truly am in Christ:

Neil T. Anderson

Barbara Yoder

Benjamin Deitrick

Dr. Douglas E. Carr

Dr. Bernardine Daniels

Patricia King

Rosie Wagner

Most I know personally, others I have gleaned extensively from their publications and public ministry. I appreciate each one immensely.

Also, a big "thank you" to Emma and Mia Gauthier, two very special young ladies who are up and coming change-makers, who love Jesus, for designing and drawing free-hand several illustrations in this book. Your contribution to the Kingdom does not go unnoticed. May you be blessed coming in and going out and may the presence of the Lord surround you always. You are loved!

Endnotes

[1] Oxford Languages, Google.com

[2] "Finally, my brethren, be strong in the Lord and in the power of His might. Put on the whole armor of God, that you may be able to stand against the wiles of the devil. For we do not wrestle against flesh and blood, but against principalities, against powers, against the rulers of the darkness of this age, against spiritual hosts of wickedness in the heavenly places" (Ephesians 6:10-12 NKJV).

www.ingramcontent.com/pod-product-compliance
Lightning Source LLC
Chambersburg PA
CBHW070856050426
42453CB00012B/2230